Y0-AFY-251

NEW YORK AND MID-ATLANTIC

The Black Bass Hotel, Lumberville

COUNTRY INNS OF AMERICA

New York

AND

Mid-Atlantic

A GUIDE TO THE INNS OF
NEW YORK, DELAWARE, MARYLAND, NEW JERSEY, AND PENNSYLVANIA

BY PETER ANDREWS AND TRACY ECCLESINE

DESIGNED BY ROBERT REID

HOLT, RINEHART AND WINSTON, *New York*
THE KNAPP PRESS, *Los Angeles*

Frontispiece photograph
The Ruskin Room at the Roycroft Inn,
by George W. Gardner.

Copyright © 1980 by Knapp
Communications Corporation.
Published in the United States of
America in 1980 by the Knapp Press,
5900 Wilshire Boulevard, Los Angeles,
California 90036, and by
Holt, Rinehart and Winston,
383 Madison Avenue, New York,
New York 10017.
Published simultaneously by
Holt, Rinehart and Winston
of Canada, Limited.
All rights reserved, including the
right to reproduce this book or
portions thereof in any form.

Library of Congress Cataloging in Publication Data
Andrews, Peter, 1931–
    Country inns of America.

    Vol. 3 by P. Andrews and T. Ecclesine; vol. 4 by
P. Andrews and G. Allen.
    CONTENTS: [1] Upper New England.—[2] Lower New
England.—[3] New York and Mid-Atlantic.—[4] California.
    1. Hotels, taverns, etc.—California—Directories.
I. Allen, George, 1936–   joint author.
II. Ecclesine, Tracy, joint author.   III. Reid, Robert,
1927–   IV. Title.
TX907.A662   647′.94′73   79-22906
ISBN 0 03 043721 0

10 9 8 7 6 5 4

A Robert Reid-Wieser & Wieser production
Printed in U.S.A. by R. R. Donnelley & Sons

ISBN 0-03-043721-0

CONTENTS

Photographed by Lilo Raymond

All other inns photographed by George W. Gardner.

EDITOR'S NOTE

There are forty inns described and illustrated in this book. Our photographers and writers visited many more, but selected these as, for various reasons, outstanding: historical interest, food, ambience, innkeepers, furnishings, and local amenities. Changes may have taken place since we were there, but each inn has its own personal mix of these characteristics, and a visit to any one should certainly be worthwhile.

Inn-goers have strong personal preferences, and different types of inns are represented so that potential guests can choose those that best suit their individual taste.

Not all of the fine inns in the region could be given the full coverage they deserve, so rather than omit them we have given condensed information in the back of the book on these others that impressed us. Inclusion in this section does not imply that these inns—some of them spectacular, some modest—are of lesser merit or appeal. And if we have omitted some personal favorites, please let us know so that we can give them a "second look" for future editions of this practical guide.

The Gold Room.

Back to basics and cheery accommodations

No maraschino cherries here, or MSG, or processed foods. It's back to basics at the Asa Ransom House, where innkeepers Bob and Judy Lenz share their concern for good health by offering a steady diet of fresh, wholesome food and cheery accommodations in a restful little town.

The inn is located in Clarence, just fifteen miles from Buffalo. The town's first white settler was a young silversmith named Asa Ransom, who in 1799 obtained title to a ten-mile lot by agreeing to build and operate a tavern.

No one knows exactly where the young Ransom built his tavern, but the remains of his gristmill, built in 1803, were found at the rear of the inn. The Lenzes named their inn after him and have been able to document it as far back as 1858. Aided by numerous antique shops, flea markets and the local historical society, the Lenzes have brought in many period items to help recall bygone days: children's notepads dating back to the 1870s, old-fashioned vacuum cleaners, copper pots and kerosene lamps.

The food has been prepared with careful attention to detail. Specials include salmon pond pie, smoked corned beef with apple-raisin sauce, roast leg of lamb and the ever popular chicken with Mornay sauce in a caraway puff. The homemade soups are luscious and are served from large kettles at the table. The homemade bread, which is first rate, comes with small scoops of honey butter, apple butter and unsalted butter. At breakfast, the cheese pie with corned beef is a lovely excuse to linger over a second cup of coffee.

Upstairs there's another small feast. Each of the four guest rooms has been supplied with a bowl of fresh fruit. The Blue Room, popular with honey-mooners, has a canopy bed with matching wallpaper, lamp shades and bedspread. Room 4 has a nice view of the inn's herb garden, a well-maintained collection of more than forty herbs and spices. The other two rooms have brass beds and a cannonball double bed.

As for activities, there is chess in the library and tennis and swimming at the nearby town park. (Note to potential guests: the inn is closed from sundown Friday to sundown Saturday because of the religious beliefs of its owners.)

A sampling of the inn's delightful desserts includes chocolate fudge pecan pie, lemon coconut cream pie and toasted butter pecan pie.

ASA RANSOM HOUSE, 10529 Main St., Clarence, N.Y. 14031; (716) 759-2315; Bob and Judy Lenz, Innkeepers. An 1858 inn with 4 guest rooms. Private baths. Open Sundays to Thursdays all year except for 2 weeks in fall and the first 3 weeks in February. Rates, $30 double; $22 single, include full breakfast. Restaurant serves dinner every day except Friday and Saturday, lunch on Wednesdays and possibly every day during summer. Children welcome; no pets. No credit cards accepted. Near town park with tennis and swimming.

DIRECTIONS: From Buffalo, take Route 5, 15 miles east. From N.Y. Thruway, take Exit 48A at Pembroke to 77 South to Route 5. Inn is about 10 miles west.

Benedict Arnold slept here

The Beekman Arms is a multifaceted inn that has been the pillar of the historic Hudson River town of Rhinebeck since 1700. Believed by many to be the oldest hotel in America, the inn has also served as a fort, a stagecoach stop, a theater, Rhinebeck's town hall, its post office and even the local newspaper office.

During his presidential campaigns, Franklin D. Roosevelt (who lived in nearby Hyde Park) made some of his liveliest campaign speeches from the inn's front porch. F.D.R. was not the first famous man to cross paths with the inn. Other earlier guests included the Marquis de Lafayette, Aaron Burr, Benedict Arnold, Alexander Hamilton, Martin Van Buren, Theodore Roosevelt, Horace Greeley, William Jennings Bryan and Benjamin Harrison.

The town of Rhinebeck is full of fascinating stories, so try to take DeWitt Gurnell's informal tour, which begins at the Beekman Arms. Gurnell, the town historian, leads you to the stark Dutch Orthodox church, where Tories were held prisoner, and to its simple graveyard, where forty-two Revolutionary War soldiers are buried. The pews have plaques dedicated to their original owners, such as General Richard Montgomery, a local landowner who drilled the Colonial militia on the Beekman Arms's front lawn, and many other Colonial figures, including a man who was excommunicated from the church for holding a funeral for his dead horse.

Nearby is the former home of two sisters who were both said to be girl friends of Aaron Burr. Another authentic item on the tour is Pocahontas Pointer, a nineteenth-century wooden fire engine that is affectionately known as "Old Pokie."

Returning to the inn, there are numerous muskets, old deeds, pewter mugs and other paraphernalia. The guest rooms are comfortable in a somewhat modernized Colonial mode, with floral wallpaper, sinks in rooms, some braided rugs and old-fashioned lamps. Many rooms have private baths.

The focal point of historic Rhinebeck for almost 300 years, the inn once doubled as a fort.

Dining in the Pewter Room.

The inn is well known for its prime ribs, and the roast duckling in Bing cherry sauce is another favorite. The menu is primarily American, with a fairly good variety of entrées. Eggplant de Carnevalle is a vegetarian dish that is gaining a following, and the café La Forge, a Kahlua and Grand Marnier drink, is also well liked by visitors.

Rhinebeck is a good town for lolling about, with its three bookstores, general stores and movie house featuring classic films. Nearby are wineries, antique shops, F.D.R.'s home, a reptile farm and the famous Rhinebeck Aerodrome.

BEEKMAN ARMS, 4 Mill St., Rhinebeck, N.Y. 12572; (914) 876-7077; Earl S. Bebo, Innkeeper. A Colonial inn in the Hudson River Valley, with 18 guest rooms. Private baths. Open all year except Christmas. Rates $28 to $32 double; $18 to $24 single. Children welcome; pets allowed. Visa, Master Charge and American Express credit cards accepted. Restaurant serves lunch, dinner and Sunday brunch. Swimming pool, tennis courts nearby.

DIRECTIONS: From New York City, take Route 9 direct to Rhinebeck. Inn is in center of town.

Peace and relaxation in the Grand Canyon of the East

Glen Iris is in the midst, and the mist, of what is popularly known as the Grand Canyon of the East, Letchworth State Park, with seventeen miles of winding canyons and breathtaking views.

Just beyond the inn's front door is the 107-foot Middle Falls, a sight that literally keeps visitors hypnotized with its churning waters almost as far as the eye can see. The falls' restful effect is universally acclaimed: many guests say that a weekend at the inn is as relaxing as a full week anywhere else.

In 1859 William Letchworth, a businessman and humanitarian, bought 1,000 acres around the falls, thus preserving it from commercialization. He lived in semiretirement for many years at what is now the inn, became active in philanthropic activities and was president of the state board of charities for ten years. At his death in 1910, his land became a state park, and today thousands can enjoy the view he once held so dear.

The Glen Iris restaurant is very successful with its primarily American menu. Innkeeper Peter Pizzutelli is a former director of the New York Restaurant Association, and he takes great pride in seeing that the menu is enticing. The seafood list is fairly extensive, along with the steaks and chops. In the dessert category, the Rebel torte, a peanut butter concoction, continues to delight visitors from all over the world.

Glen Iris's overnight accommodations are a mixed and sometimes awkward blend of new and old furniture; there are twenty-one guest rooms, seven of

A view of the falls from the upstairs hallway.

Detail of an upstairs window.

which are in a motel setting nearby. The rooms are named after the species of some 10,000 trees which Letchworth is said to have planted in the park: deodar, silver fir, Douglas fir, linden, etc.

Other inn features to ponder: a fine collection of Polish glass; old-fashioned stained glass window panels; a dark wood stairway that looks Bavarian; and the third-floor study, a collection of fascinating citations to Mr. Letchworth.

The exterior of the inn has an impressive portico that is perfect for catching the summer breeze.

GLEN IRIS INN, Letchworth State Park, Castile, N.Y. 14427; (716) 493-2622; Peter and Cora Pizzutelli, Innkeepers. A converted 1859 home, with 14 guest rooms and nearby motel with 7 guest rooms. All private baths. Open from Easter through first Sunday in Nov. Rates $22 to $29 double. Restaurant serves 3 meals. Children welcome; pets permitted in motel. Visa, Master Charge and American Express credit cards accepted. Playgrounds, swimming pools and hiking in park.

DIRECTIONS: From Buffalo, take Route 20A to Warsaw, then Route 19 South to 19A to south entrance to state park. Inn is 1 mile north of entrance.

The inn's gift shop—a potpourri of trinkets and nostalgia.

Haute cuisine is its raison d'être

The entries in the guest book tell the story. Members of the Boston Symphony wrote, "We're proud to taste the symphonies of a great artist." Robert Redford implores, "Please don't expand!"

The proprietor-chef, and chief miracle worker of L'Hostellerie Bressane, is Jean Morel, a maître de cuisine trained in his native France. He was chef at Le Chateaubriand in New York City and later at the Restaurant Lafayette in the days when Jacqueline Kennedy made it her personal preserve. Recently he was named a Master Chef of France by L'Association des Maîtres Cuisinier de France.

But he and his wife, Madeleine, grew tired of city life and eventually found just the building they were looking for to turn into a country inn. The frame house was built in 1782 and still has its Palladian windows, wide plank flooring and the original mantels. The Morels bought it in 1971, and, after adding a proper kitchen and doing other necessary work, opened for business in 1972. The *New York Times* gave them three stars. Madeleine, true to the French tradition of an innkeeper's wife, is very active in the management end.

L'Hostellerie Bressane is furnished with the Morels' own family heirlooms and unusual antiques. The four

A dessert soufflé, meticulously prepared and served.

cozy rooms upstairs have their own fireplaces, and people often reserve a room so they can enjoy a long and leisurely dinner.

The food is the raison d'être of L'Hostellerie. The service and ambience are perfect, but the food is unsurpassed. Every meal is a unique experience, and Chef Morel gives even traditional dishes his own special touch. "Everyone serves onion soup, but no one adds egg yolks, Madeira and cognac," he explains. A "*gâteau*" of chicken livers with a tomato sauce, similar to a soufflé, is a delicious appetizer from his native Bresse. The specialties, from broiled baby lobster in garlic butter to braised sweetbreads with chestnuts and port, depend to a large extent on what is in season. Chef Morel selects his own produce every day; the turbot is flown in from France, and the meat is driven up from New York City. There are no shortcuts in his kitchen, and he uses only premier grade wines in cooking. All the breads, soup stocks, sauces and pastries are made from scratch, including the warm croissants for breakfast.

The Morels close the inn for two months in the early part of each year and return to France. Keeping up with what's going on in the world of haute cuisine is Jean Morel's life work—and L'Hostellerie Bressane benefits tremendously by his dedication. As he says, "In our little hotel, everything must be first class."

All wines, even those used in cooking, are of premium grade.

The welcome mat is always out at this superb French oasis in upstate New York.

L'HOSTELLERIE BRESSANE, P.O. Box 268, Hillsdale, New York 12529; (518) 325-3412, Jean Morel, Innkeeper. A 4-room inn, with an internationally famous restaurant, on the Hudson River. Closed February and March. Room rates are $23 for single or double occupancy. Shared baths. Restaurant serves dinner. No credit cards accepted.

DIRECTIONS: Located at the intersection of N.Y. 22 and N.Y. 23, on the east side of the Hudson River, 110 miles north of New York City.

One of the best-known country inns in America

The Old Drover's Inn was built over a natural spring in 1750 by two brothers who named it the Clearwater Tavern. They were Quakers and had hoped to run an abstemious establishment, but their regular customers, a bunch of rough-and-ready drovers from upstate New York on their way to New York City with their herds of livestock, wanted something stronger than clear water when they arrived. The brothers could not bring themselves to actually dispense liquor, so they made an interesting compromise by placing a keg of rum by the fireplace with a sign on it saying, "Drink what ye will. Pay what ye may."

More than 200 years later, the inn is still catering to thirsty (and hungry) travelers, but nowadays they are the carriage trade. Bought in 1937 by Olin Chester Potter and renamed Old Drover's Inn, it has become one of the best-known country inns in America. Still owned by the Potter family, it is managed by innkeeper Travis Harris, who has been here thirty years. "I grew up with the inn," he says, "and in all that time there have not been many changes. We've kept it pretty much the way it's always been."

The low-ceilinged taproom, with dark, gleaming paneling, hung with a wealth of period paintings and other art objects, looks as if New York City's 21 Club has gone out to the country for the weekend. The combination dining room and bar is centered by the seventeen-by-seventeen-foot chimney, which makes up the core of the house. Deviled eggs, deliciously sprinkled with hickory salt, are always served with the mammoth, fifteen-ounce cocktails. The menu is brought on a blackboard, which is then clipped to one of the low rafters, and among the house specialties are Cheddar cheese soup, stuffed partridge which are specially raised for the inn, and a light raspberry and cassis sherbet.

For the inn's guests, the day starts with specially made sausage and blueberry griddle cakes served at the six mahogany tables in the Federal Room on the first floor. Also used for private parties, the room is

Mural in the Federal Room.

decorated with rich paneling set off by red banquettes and a pastoral mural by Edward Paine. The book-lined library across the hall is a cozy sitting room with chintz-covered chairs and louvered windows.

Upstairs, cheery fires are lit in the guest rooms in the winter just before the guests' arrival, and puffy down quilts are placed at the foot of each bed. The Meeting Room, where town meetings used to be held, is the largest, sunny and yellow with a vaulted ceiling.

Travis estimates that in his time at the inn at least 8 million deviled eggs have been served, and although there is no longer a keg or sign by the fireplace, welcome is written everywhere at Old Drover's Inn.

OLD DROVER'S INN, Dover Plains, New York 12522; (914) 832-9311, Travis Harris, Innkeeper. A 3-room inn midway between New York City and the Berkshires. Closed Tuesdays and Wednesdays, and for three weeks in December. Double occupancy rates range from $50 to $70. Restaurant serves breakfast (to inn guests only), lunch and dinner. No credit cards accepted.

DIRECTIONS: Located on Old Drover's Road, off N.Y. 22, 4 miles north of Wingdale.

Sinking into overstuffed library chairs is just one of the inn's many pleasures. OVERLEAF. *Left:* this quiet spot was once a tavern for rough-and-tumble drovers. *Right:* the Taproom.

Elbert Hubbard's dream lives again

Elbert Hubbard was a successful business executive with the Larkin Soap Company, and one of the pioneers in developing mass-marketing techniques. He decided to become a writer and publisher, and in 1894 he launched his third career by establishing an independent guild of artisans, known as the Roycrofters, to create fine books and pursue other crafts.

His home, now the Roycroft Inn, was the center of a bustling campus which included a print shop, furniture studio, blacksmith house, copper shop, and power house, which furnished energy for the entire Roycroft campus. Many of the Roycroft artisans lived at the Hubbard home, and they continued to stay after Hubbard's untimely death in 1915, when he perished on the Lusitania.

Elbert Hubbard II kept his father's dream alive for more than two decades, until 1938 when the Great Depression took another toll and Hubbard was forced to close. The Hubbard home was little more than a boarding house when local restaurateurs Frank and Kitty Turgeon bought it a few years ago.

Stained glass crafted by an original Roycroft artist.

But like the original founder, the Turgeons had a dream—to restore the Roycroft campus and name to its original position in the arts. The Turgeons did extensive research into Hubbard's writings and began a massive restoration which has involved conversion of Hubbard's home into a country inn and revitalization of the old artisan's buildings, many of which are now shops.

The main rooms of the inn have a fine collection of old Roycroft pieces—solid square oak furniture that has been branded with the Roycroft R. Many of the inn's windows have stained glass panels which were made by one of the original Roycrofters. And the old permanent artists' apartments are slowly being converted into guest rooms with burlap-covered walls and matchstick bamboo blinds, as described in Hubbard's writings.

The food is of the meat and potatoes variety, heavy on the beef, and is of the same high quality that marks the 13 other Turgeon-owned restaurants in Western New York and Houston.

Under the direction of Hubbard's granddaughter, a group of craftsmen called the Roycrofters are producing new works, striving to maintain the high standards of the original Roycrofters. Hubbard would be pleased and gratified that, thanks to the Turgeons, his home looks like its old self again and is, in his own words, "devoted to the business of living."

Roycroft Gift Shop—center for high quality local crafts. OVERLEAF. *Left:* Ruskin Room, 3rd floor museum of Elbert Hubbard's books, manuscripts, pottery, and furniture. *Right:* Alice's Office, former headquarters for Hubbard's wife, is now used for small parties.

ROYCROFT INN, 40 South Grove Street, East Aurora, New York 14052; (716) 652-9030, Frank and Kitty Turgeon, Innkeepers. The complex includes guest accommodations, craft workshops, restaurant and shop. Open all year. Double occupancy rates range from $28 to $36. Restaurant serves breakfast, lunch and dinner. American Express, Master Charge and Visa credit cards accepted.

DIRECTIONS: Approximately 12 miles east of Buffalo, the inn is located off Main Street, near the Town Hall.

"We have a lot of millionaires . . . but they're nice millionaires"

The Shandaken Inn is a weekend getaway that is used almost exclusively by friends and acquaintances of Gisele Mallory and Albert Pollack.

Begun two years ago by the couple, who had left their New York careers (his in the record business and hers in interior decorating), the Shandaken Inn functions very much like a private party. Guests are generally not taken in unless they have been recommended by other guests.

But for those who do know a friend of a friend of a friend, the inn has a lot to recommend itself. Gisele, an effervescent Frenchwoman, and Albert, who resembles Paul Newman and who might know about fifty French words, are excellent hosts who are always making sure their guests are having a good time. The entertainment begins with a cocktail, served as soon as each guest crosses the threshold from a sunken bar in the middle of the sprawling living room. Albert, likely as not, will be making the drinks himself.

The inn, once a dairy barn, was built around 1880 and later turned into a nine-hole golf club. John Philip Sousa was said to be a charter member. The club closed during the crash of '29 and was reopened as a boardinghouse eight years later. Gisele and Albert bought the inn in 1974 as a country house; their friends visited on weekends, brought friends, and before they knew it they had a country inn on their hands.

Shandaken is five miles from the Belleayre ski area, and in winter the inn has kind of a tony ski house atmosphere, the clientele tends to be the low-key jet set variety. As Albert says, "We have a lot of millionaires here, but they're nice millionaires." On Saturday night the inn becomes a minidisco when Albert disappears into his small recording studio and the music begins.

Meanwhile Gisele is recovering from her labors in the kitchen. She is a self-confessed perfectionist, and her country French cuisine is usually very tasty. The menu is simple, with one entrée each evening topped off by an elegant dessert like a raspberry tart. After

Raspberry tarts are *une grande specialité de la maison.*

dinner she appears in a fancy dress and makes sure that her guests have enjoyed their dinners.

Guest rooms are comfortable, clean, unpretentious and have a somewhat modern feeling to them. Gisele has placed many interesting objects around the house to admire—petit points, quilts and artwork—but the saddle in the upstairs hall is probably the crowning item in what is a very individual inn.

THE SHANDAKEN INN, Golf Course Rd., Shandaken, N.Y. 12480; (914) 688-5100; Albert Pollack and Gisele Mallory, Innkeepers. A nineteenth-century inn with 12 guest rooms. Private baths. Inn is open all year on weekends only, except for 2 weeks in April and the first 3 weeks in November. Reopens Thanksgiving. Rates $95 double; $65 single, plus a 15% service charge. All rates include Continental breakfast and dinner. In summer, inn guests may lunch by the swimming pool at an extra charge. Restaurant open for dinner by advance reservation only. Children not accepted. Pets permitted at the discretion of the innkeepers. No credit cards accepted. Swimming pool, tennis court, fishing.

DIRECTIONS: From N.Y. Thruway, take Kingston Exit 19. After the tollbooth, take first right at the traffic circle onto Route 28 and follow for 29 miles to inn.

A former dairy barn is now the attractive home of The Shandaken Inn.

A well-loved inn in beautiful East Hampton

Trim and white with green shutters, the 1770 House stands on the main street of East Hampton, often called "the most beautiful village in America." Guests of the inn and restaurant would find it hard to disagree. Next door is the original town hall, built in 1731; and next to that is what was once the Clinton Academy, the first academic institution in the state.

During its long life, the 1770 House has been a general store, a private home, an annex of the Clinton Academy, a boardinghouse and now an inn. During the late 1940s and 1950s, it was popular with actors, including Clark Gable, who appeared at the John Drew Theater across the street. By the late 1960s, the charming old place had fallen on hard times. It was saved by Sidney and Miriam Perle, who were looking for a country inn as a means to semiretirement. Sidney was a successful clothing retailer, and Miriam had had her own cooking school and catering business; but they soon discovered there is no such thing as "semiretirement" in being an innkeeper. They put in months of hard work getting it all together, and the refurbished rooms are now a setting for the Perles' many nineteenth-century antiques, as well as their fine period clock collection.

On one wall is a portrait Miriam did herself. "I needed a Colonial ancestor for the place, so I painted one of my own." The dining room walls are a chocolate brown, and the bright white woodwork and white, bamboo-patterned Regency chairs keep the room light and airy. Each of the six guest rooms, all with baths, has its own dominant color, and the brown tones in a front guest room with a double four-poster canopied in beige are warm and inviting.

A Cordon Bleu graduate, Miriam runs the large kitchen, where she also gives cooking classes. Her eclectic "cuisine of today" includes a fabulous quiche, blintzes Florentine, vacherin cassis and an outstanding whiskey cake. The inn's menu is constantly varied, and the Perles' daughter Wendy is the pastry chef. Their son Adam tends bar in the Colonial Taproom, a year-round favorite.

Restoring an old house involves many surprises, and although the Perles had thought the house was built in 1770, a beehive oven they found in the cellar probably dates from the 1730s. But the most important date for the 1770 House must be when the Perles undertook its restoration as a country inn. For now, once again, it can take its rightful place among its distinguished and well-maintained neighbors in the lovely old town of East Hampton.

The inn is one of the oldest buildings in a historic Long Island village. One of six color-coordinated guest rooms, all with private baths. OVERLEAF. *Left:* part of the inn's unusual brass collection. *Right:* cuisine is as sparkling as this Regency chandelier.

1770 HOUSE, 143 Main Street, East Hampton, New York 11937; (516) 324-1770, Sidney and Miriam Perle, Innkeepers. A 6-room inn located in a Long Island resort town. Open all year. Restaurant open on weekends only during the winter. Double occupancy rates: June through October $49 and $59; November through May $40 and $49, including Continental breakfast. Restaurant serves dinner; Taproom serves refreshments after the theater during the summer. Major credit cards are accepted.

DIRECTIONS: N.Y. 27 to East Hampton on Long Island. The inn is located just beyond the village green, on the left, beyond the cupola-topped Clinton Museum.

Good food and theater in Finger Lakes country

Two hundred years ago, the Cayuga Indians at Owasco Lake called it the Great Spring. Today that same pond graces the front lawn of The Springside Inn—a historic old inn in New York's Finger Lakes country.

During the past century and a half, this large three-story inn has led many lives: it has been a day school, part of the underground railway, a private home, and it now doubles as a summer dinner theater, featuring hits from Broadway. The theater idea was the inspiration of innkeepers Bill and Barbara Dove, who both have acting backgrounds.

Each performance is prefaced by a dinner repertoire that has been lovingly perfected over the past eight years. As Barbara says, "We're food people. We'll never get rich because we put all our money into food."

Bob supervises the kitchen, whose specialties include lobster Newburg, roast Long Island duckling à l'orange and filet of sole Florentine. Marinated mushrooms and cheese soufflés are an enticing part of the daily fare, and during dinner, things like fresh hot popovers and banana bread have a way of appearing at the table.

On Sunday afternoons, the inn offers its "family dinner"—baked chicken, roast beef and baked Virginia ham, with chicken soup as an appetizer, and homemade ice cream with homemade toppings for making your own sundaes. The main dining room, with its cathedral ceiling, massive beams and turn-of-the-century hanging lamps, is usually pretty well packed. Many wedding receptions and banquets are held at the inn's East Porch, which has a lovely view of the pond.

The inn's seven guest rooms have been done in a variety of modes, ranging from Victorian to semi-modern. Fresh paint has been applied liberally, and

Genuine country décor.

the effect is cheery, from the red doors to wide-planked black floors.

The Finger Lakes offer many activities for the traveler, and nearby there are wineries, state parks, antique and country stores and the William Henry Seward House (home of the secretary of state under Lincoln and Andrew Johnson). In winter the inn has cross-country skiing, and there are several downhill ski areas within an hour's drive.

THE SPRINGSIDE INN, Route 38 South, Auburn, N.Y. 13021; (315) 252-7247; Bill and Barbara Dove, Innkeepers. A 7-guest room inn and restaurant in the beautiful Finger Lakes. Private and shared baths. Open all year except Mondays, Memorial Day through Labor Day. Closed rest of year on Mondays and Tuesdays. Rates $18 single; $28 double, including Continental breakfast. Children welcome; pets accepted at discretion of innkeepers. Visa and Master Charge credit cards accepted. Dinner theater open during July and Aug. $14.95 per person for dinner and show. Swimming and boating on lake; golf and riding nearby.

DIRECTIONS: From N. Y. Thruway, take Exit 40. Follow Route 34 South to Route 38 South. Bear left at traffic circle onto West Lake Rd. Drive ¼ mile to inn.

A century ago, runaway slaves gathered in the woods behind this historic Finger Lakes inn. It was named after a pond which Indians called the Great Spring.

Majestic Victoriana with down-home atmosphere

Up the hill from the busy college town of Ithaca is the majestic Taughannock Farms Inn in Trumansburg, New York. A sweeping three-story Victorian building, the inn was once the main house of a gentleman's farm of more than 400 acres.

Today the farm is broken up and much of the land given over to neighboring Taughannock State Park. So instead of overlooking the farm, the inn now looks down on a wide patch of green where Frisbee players and kite flyers have a heyday in the afternoon. Beyond the green are Cayuga Lake, Cornell University and Ithaca College. The inn has become a favorite stopping place for university visitors, college presidents, professors and a best-selling novelist or two.

But no matter how illustrious its guests, the inn is basically a down-home place. "We don't want to be pretentious," says innkeeper Keith le Grand, speaking about the cuisine. "We don't put fancy titles on things."

The menu is wholesome American fare, Long Island duckling with orange sauce and roast leg of lamb the most popular items. The dessert list is ex-

Upstairs sitting room is furnished with finds from attic.

tensive, and one favorite, the crème de menthe parfait—a cooling swirl of green and white topped by a cherry—has been in Nancy le Grand's family for three generations, about as long as they have had the inn. Her seventy-year-old grandmother Maude is the "resident taste bud" in charge of the kitchen. Sunday dinner seems to attract more than a few of Maude's contemporaries.

The inn has four dining rooms with large connecting windows that overlook the park and the lake. The forsythia bloom by the flagstone walk outside, and there are plenty of spots to admire the ginkgo trees or darting butterflies. Down the road are Taughannock Falls, which at 215 feet are higher than Niagara Falls.

The guest rooms are medium to large, airy and somewhat varied. They have marble-topped sinks, floral wallpapers, Victorian headboards, and all but one room share baths. Keith and Nancy keep trucking down their Victorian finds from the attic, placing them in just the right spots to add a touch of interest to the various rooms. The sitting rooms upstairs are almost too nicely furnished to be used.

The bedrooms may be a bit drafty on colder nights, so ask for extra blankets. The inn is open from Easter to Thanksgiving, and reservations are advised.

Dining room fare is well-prepared American food.

Far above Cayuga's waters is this majestic inn—a former gentleman's farm of some 400 acres. OVERLEAF: the falls in nearby Taughannock State Park provide solace and exhilaration on a hot summer day.

TAUGHANNOCK FARMS INN, Route 89 at Gorge Rd., Trumansburg, N.Y. 14886; (607) 387-7711; Keith and Nancy le Grand, Innkeepers. Victorian home, adjacent to Taughannock Falls State Park, with 4 guest rooms. One private bath; other rooms share. Open Easter to Thanksgiving. Rates $18 to $22 single; $22 to $26 double. Breakfast served to inn guests only. Dinner served on weeknights and on Sunday at 1:00 P.M. Children welcome; no pets. No credit cards accepted. All park recreational facilities; boat tours of lake in summer to view falls.

DIRECTIONS: From Ithaca, take Route 89 North. Inn is 8 miles on the left.

Early Americana on the Long Island coast

Stony Brook is an old seafaring town with a natural harbor that has been active since pre-Revolutionary War days. And thanks to Stony Brook's concerned citizens, along with financial help from the Ward Melville family, the town has retained its Early American flavor.

The village has many historic homes and sites: the Three Village Inn, built in 1785, was once the home of Jonas Smith, Long Island's first millionaire. Smith was a shipbuilder who constructed many of his ships by the marina behind the inn. Across the street from the inn is Hercules, a figurehead from the U.S.S. *Ohio,* Admiral Farragut's flagship. Stony Brook's main street has a uniform one-story weathered gray façade, crowned by a colorful wooden eagle on the post office, which flaps its wings every day at noon.

Nearby is the Suffolk Museum featuring pictures of Early American settlers, Long Island wildlife and paintings by William Sidney Mount, a well-known local artist. The Suffolk Museum carriage house has a very fine collection of horse-drawn vehicles, and for architectural buffs, there is Stony Brook's Episcopal church, designed by Stanford White. The gristmill is on a side road and attracts ducks and other wildlife that are favorites of both tourists and local residents.

The Three Village Inn is a two-story white clapboard structure that offers a variety of accommodations: a few old-fashioned guest rooms in the main house and several cottages out back overlooking the sandy beach and marina. The rooms in the cottages are a little motel-like, with many modern conveniences, while those in the main house have a bit more Old World charm, with their beamed ceilings, wide-planked floors and old-fashioned furniture. But from every room there is a bright view almost any time of the year.

Downstairs, the view from the front dining rooms is equally pleasant. The inn does a brisk luncheon business, serving buffet-style meals as well as a large selection of sandwiches and heartier entrées. As might be expected, seafood is very popular, and many kinds are served: clams, weakfish with capers, bluefish

amandine, oysters, Peconic Bay scallops, Maine lobster, rainbow trout with pine nuts, filet of flounder in white wine, swordfish with grilled tomato, as well as steamers and soft-shell crabs. Banana cake, cider and spiced fruit, complimentary with dinner, are served at appropriate intervals.

The inn has a nice mix of dining areas: a room for nonsmokers, the Sandbar Room (done in pink), an intimate room with a fireplace and the Candlelight Room behind the bar, all in wood.

THREE VILLAGE INN, Dock Rd., Stony Brook, N.Y. 11790; (516) 751-0555; Nelson and Monda Roberts, Innkeepers. An Early American inn on Long Island with 24 guest rooms (including one for disabled persons). Private baths. Open all year except Christmas. Rates $20 to $40 single; $35 to $50 double. Children welcome; no pets. Restaurant serves 3 meals daily. Visa, Master Charge and American Express credit cards accepted. Adjacent to town beach; tennis, golf nearby.

DIRECTIONS: From L. I. Expressway, take Exit 62 to end of Nichols Rd. North. Turn left at traffic light, continue to next traffic light and turn right onto Main St. straight ahead to inn. In summer, a car ferry runs from Bridgeport, Ct. to Port Jefferson, 15 minutes from Stony Brook.

The eighteenth-century inn was once the home of ship builder Jonas Smith, Long Island's first millionaire. The restaurant, below, has an extensive seafood list.

Nothing fancy: just simple food in an old-time inn

Cooperstown is one of those American tourist spots that virtually has something for everyone.

For baseball lovers, there's the Baseball Hall of Fame, where visitors can see everything from Babe Ruth's locker to Lou Gehrig's uniform to old-time catchers' mitts to Willie Mays's shiny new plaque.

For those passionate about American folk art, there's the Fenimore House, with its wood carvings, metalwork, needlepoint and scrimshaw. And readers of the *Leatherstocking Tales* can pore over manuscripts from James Fenimore Cooper, whose family, incidentally, founded the town.

Those who have wondered how a blacksmith pounds out a nail or a weaver threads a loom can learn at the Farmers' Museum nearby, with craft demonstrations and museum exhibits dedicated to every aspect of rural life.

Cooperstown also has an ancient Indian mound, a carriage and harness museum and, perched along Otsego Lake, numerous homes and cottages dating back at least a century.

A few blocks from the Baseball Hall of Fame, the Tunnicliff is another very American institution.

In the center of town is an older building that has been a favorite hangout for locals and out-of-towners for close to 200 years: The Tunnicliff Inn. It's a small-town place, where the Lions or Rotary clubbers meet and sing their lunchtime songs a couple of times each week. There is nothing fancy about The Tunnicliff Inn. Some people might say it is a blend of old-fashioned and kitsch. Nevertheless, it has appeal.

The downstairs restaurant is an old stone cellar that does a brisk luncheon business. Breakfast and lunch, the only meals, are strictly short order—salads and sandwiches that are simple and fast, saving you plenty of time to roam around town.

The twenty-two guest rooms range from singles to suites that are cozy and homelike. Scattered throughout the rooms and landings are some interesting bureaus and chests that will take you back a generation or two. And being in the home of baseball you just might recall that in those days the letters *ERA* were exclusively baseball lingo.

Yes, times have changed, but The Tunnicliff Inn may well remain timeless. One final note: nightlife is almost nonexistent in Cooperstown, so be prepared with your own entertainment.

Guests relaxing in the cellar pub.

The dining room is a favorite spot for local groups. Rotary Club medals are at right.

TUNNICLIFF INN, 34-36 Pioneer St., Cooperstown, N.Y. 13326; (607) 547-9611; Magdalene Frank, Innkeeper. A 108-year-old inn with 22 guest rooms. Private baths. Open all year except Sundays. Rates $18 single; $30 double. Restaurant serves breakfast and lunch. Children welcome; pets accepted at discretion of innkeeper. No credit cards accepted. Cooperstown is home of famed baseball museum. Swimming and boating on nearby lake.

DIRECTIONS: From Albany, take Route 7 West to Colliersville. Turn right onto Route 28 North and follow to Cooperstown. Inn is in the center of town.

Traditional comfort in a tranquil outpost

When William Penn first set foot in the New World in 1682 it was on the shores of New Castle, a busy outpost on the Delaware River. Penn formally took possession of his new territory in a symbolic ceremony called "Livery of Seizin', " in which he was presented with turf, twig, soil and water.

Today, thanks to a fortunate accident, the site of that memorable ceremony has been preserved, along with the entire 300-year-old town. Because modern transportation lines bypassed New Castle in favor of nearby Wilmington, New Castle never developed. Today it is a hodgepodge of old brick buildings and cobblestone streets that conjure up a host of legends as fascinating as the town itself.

Founded in 1651 by Dutchman Peter Stuyvesant as Fort Casimir, New Castle was a choice property that caught the eye of many European powers. During its first thirty years, New Castle was ruled by the Dutch three times, the English twice and the Swedes once. It later became Delaware's first capital and was active during the Revolution.

George Read and Thomas McKean, two of Delaware's three Declaration of Independence signers, were New Castle residents; George Ross, a signer from Pennsylvania, was born in New Castle. Read's grave, as well as those of numerous other early Delaware luminaries, is at the Immanuel Church on Market Street, the site of Penn's famous "Livery of Seizin' " ceremony.

In the heart of town is the New Castle Courthouse, an impressive brick structure whose striking white cupola formed the center of the circle creating the Mason-Dixon Line, the legendary boundary between the Northern and Southern states.

Almost directly across from the courthouse is a four-guest-room brick home which is colloquially

Immanuel Churchyard. Burial place for George Read, signer of the Declaration of Independence.

A corner of the living room.

known as the William Penn Guest House. There's actually no such listing in the telephone book, nor any such sign out front. The only indication that the building at 206 Delaware Street is any different from its neighbors is a small sign marked "Guests."

The guest house is a favorite among urbanites from nearby Wilmington, Washington and Baltimore, who sometimes visit three or four times a year to escape back a few centuries in time. Guest rooms are old-fashioned and simple, with braided rugs and wide planked floors. Air conditioning and television are available, but most guests don't need them.

The inn does not serve meals, but New Castle has two restaurants and a coffee shop and there are many dining places in nearby Wilmington.

WILLIAM PENN GUEST HOUSE, 206 Delaware St., New Castle, Del. 19720; (302) 328-7736; Mr. and Mrs. Richard Burwell, Innkeepers. A 1682 brick home in a historic Delaware town. 4 guest rooms. Open all year. $15 per room per night. Shared baths. No meals. Children permitted, but no pets. No credit cards accepted.

DIRECTIONS: From I-95, follow signs to New Castle which lead into Delaware Street.

The formal dining room.

"Find peace in a violent world. . . . Go fishing . . . make friends"

The Chesapeake House, with twelve boats for charter daily, is headquarters for one of the largest sportfishing fleets on Chesapeake Bay. And although the sportfishing operation may be well known to fishing enthusiasts, the restaurant and inn are still a bit of a secret.

"We're at the other end of the world, almost," explains Mrs. Levin Harrison, Jr., the owner, speaking of the inn's location on a quiet little island. "People sometimes drive over from the mainland, and they're so surprised to find us. 'I wish I'd known about you *before,*' they say. 'I would have stayed with you.'"

For those who have discovered the inn, which is open from April to November, the food is a big attraction. The sautéed lump crab meat, baked with butter and sliced ham, is especially tasty. The oysters on the half shell have a flavor that is unmatched, and the other seafood dishes are usually excellent. From time to time, the chef serves special oyster dishes, and the oysters wrapped with bacon and broiled until crisp are sparkling little items that Mrs. Harrison calls angels on horseback.

Vegetables, generally fresh and ranging from stewed tomatoes (an old family recipe) and kale to mashed potatoes and cole slaw, are served in family-style bowls along with homemade bread.

Guest rooms are spread throughout the main house and in ten adjoining motel units. The older rooms share baths, are simply decorated with white bedspreads, and are clean and comfortable. Several suites are available in the house. The motel units have private baths.

The sportfishing business has mushroomed during the past fifty years, and more and more women and children are joining the men on the boats. Buddy Harrison, Mrs. Harrison's son, is in command of the fleet, and he offers special rates to children under twelve.

For an interesting side trip, drive up the road to see some of the very few skipjacks in the United States: sailing ships that are used for oystering. Skipjacking is almost a forgotten way of life, and the sight of the ships and their leather-faced captains brings to mind a time when life was a lot simpler. As Buddy likes to say, "Find peace in a violent world. Go fishing and make friends."

HARRISON'S CHESAPEAKE HOUSE, Tilghman, Md. 21671; (301) 886-2123; Mrs. Levin Harrison, Jr., Innkeeper. An 1860 inn with 22 guest rooms and restaurant on Chesapeake Bay. Private and shared baths. Adjacent motel has 10 guest rooms with private baths. Open from end of April to Thanksgiving. Rates in inn, $35 per person with 3 meals; $30 double, weekends, without meals; $25 double, weekdays, without meals. In motel, $40 per person with 3 meals; $30 double, weekdays, without meals; $37 double, weekends, without meals. Children under 12 half price. No pets. No credit cards accepted. Fishing and swimming at inn; tennis and golf nearby.

DIRECTIONS: From Annapolis, take Route 50 across Chesapeake Bay Bridge into Easton. One-half mile beyond airport, take Easton Bypass 322 to Route 33. Inn is ½ mile beyond bridge at Tilghman on left-hand side.

A favorite spot for trading fish stories.

Good jazz and Chesapeake Bay cuisine

Just a stone's throw from the governor's mansion is The Maryland Inn, a Colonial hostelry that has been an integral part of the historic city of Annapolis since the eighteenth century.

The statehouse, built in 1772, is now the nation's oldest statehouse in continuous use. It was in Annapolis, in 1784, that Congress ratified the Treaty of Paris, ending the Revolutionary War. And in Annapolis that George Washington resigned his commission as commander-in-chief of the Continental Army.

The Maryland Inn sits in the center of the city's landmark historic district, and for 200 years it has been a convenient and well-liked spot for prominent national, state and naval visitors. With the Naval Academy and historic buildings, Annapolis has become a low-key tourist center.

To cater to the interest in Chesapeake Bay cuisine, The Maryland Inn provides a large selection of seafood dishes. The most popular entrée, known as the Treaty of Paris, is an aromatic array featuring scallops, crab meat, langouste and shrimp, prepared with wine and herbs. The Chesapeake salad with crab meat and langouste on a bed of crisp greens, garnished with white asparagus, tomato wedges and hard-boiled eggs, is a tender mingling of flavors. And the Maryland crab bisque, a house specialty, is thick and deliciously seasoned.

Meanwhile, for jazz lovers, the inn presents an ex-

citing program in the King of France Room, which was restored in consultation with guitarist Charlie Byrd, who is the resident guest artist. Besides Byrd, the inn has brought in numerous other top jazz performers, including Earl Hines, Gap Mangione and Monty Alexander.

The twenty-two guest rooms are different. Many have a view of the statehouse or other Colonial buildings, and all have air conditioning, telephones, televisions and private baths.

MARYLAND INN, Church Circle, Annapolis, Md. 21401; (301) 263-2641; Paul Pearson, Innkeeper. A landmark inn, with 44 rooms, restored to Victorian splendor. Private baths. Open all year. Rates $28 to $40 single; $34 to $49 double. Suites $57 to $75. The fine restaurant serves 3 meals daily, with the emphasis on seafood. Children welcome; pets allowed. Visa, Master Charge and American Express credit cards accepted. Many historic sites nearby; tours of the U.S. Naval Academy.

DIRECTIONS: From Washington, take Route 50 East to Annapolis Naval Academy exit. Continue to Church Circle. From Baltimore, take Route 2 South to first directional turn-off marked Washington/Annapolis. Continue to Church Circle.

Charlie Byrd, noted jazz guitarist and resident artist at the inn.

Annapolis Statehouse—oldest continuously operating capitol building in the nation.

A formal country inn in tidewater country

The first Robert Morris in Oxford came to the New World in 1738 and arrived in the bustling Maryland seaport to take charge of the American end of a British tobacco importing company. He quickly became the community's leading citizen, taking up residence in the distinguished mansion that still bears his name, and he founded one of the most important families in colonial America.

Fortunately, the original Morris family home has been lovingly preserved and maintained as one of the nation's most famous country inns. According to local legend, the house was built by ships' carpenters, and the wood-pegged wall panels bespeak its nautical heritage. The detail work throughout the inn recalls the really remarkable legacy of American craftsmen. The tavern's slate floor was quarried in Vermont, and the Morris family's coat of arms was carved in deep relief from a magnificent, single piece of oak. The four scenes depicted in the dining room—the plains of West Point, an Indian village in Winnipeg, Boston Harbor and the Natural Bridge in Virginia—are all nineteenth-century wallpapers, printed from more than 1,600 woodcuts.

Thanks to innkeepers Ken and Wendy Gibson, the Robert Morris Inn has been converted into a completely modern facility without losing one jot of its original colonial luster. The bedrooms, typical of the style of those days, tend to be a bit quixotic. There are no telephones in any of the rooms, and some of them must share a bath; but each, often with its own fireplace, is a delight in its own way.

The restaurant is one of the most famous on the Eastern Shore of Maryland. Oysters à la Gino, an exotic combination of oysters on the half-shell, topped with seasoned crabmeat and broiled with a

One of the antique woodcut wallpaper murals.

strip of bacon, is imitated, but never equaled, in kitchens all over the state.

A great variety of people are familiar with the Robert Morris, a somewhat formal country inn in the historic tidewater country. Hunters looking for ducks and geese come in the fall, and yachtsmen come any time of the year that it isn't iced over. Situated directly on the Tred Avon River, the inn has its own anchorage, and many guests miss the traffic on the highways by sailing up from Chesapeake Bay. Once they arrive here, the atmosphere is quiet and the bustle of city life far away.

ROBERT MORRIS INN, Oxford, Maryland 21654; (301) 226-5111, Kenneth and Wendy Gibson, Innkeepers. A 34-room inn with 1 cottage on the Tred Avon River. Open all year except Christmas day. Single and double occupancy rates are the same and range from $20 to $60; most private baths, some shared. The rate for the cottage, which accommodates 5, is $56. An apartment for 5 is available at $60. Restaurant serves breakfast, lunch and dinner. American Express, Master Charge and Visa charge cards accepted.

DIRECTIONS: From Easton, follow Md. 333 to the end, about six miles. The inn is on the right.

Third floor bedroom, a sunny spot under the Mansard roof.

Innkeepers Jane and Ed Rossig beneath early portraits of their children.

History, romance and breakfast in bed

When Ed and Jane Rossig, owners of The Strawberry Inn, wanted to build a log cabin in their backyard, they were surprised to discover they had received New Market's first building permit since 1918.

A sleepy little town in western Maryland, New Market is a landmark that was once a major stopping point for stagecoaches heading west. These days the old rinky-dink taverns and rundown hotels have vanished. In their place is a collection of superbly restored homes and antique shops.

Virtually every other building on Main Street is an antique store. There are forty-six in all, surely a record total for such a small town. During the week, New Market is a quiet, tightly run town, but on weekends it is a different story, with crowds of antique bargain hunters from nearby Washington and Gettysburg swelling into the streets.

The Strawberry Inn, with its three cozy guest rooms, has the only overnight lodging in town. New Market has no restaurants to speak of, and day-trippers and overnighters are usually directed to nearby Frederick for their meals. But what The Strawberry Inn lacks in cuisine, it more than makes up for in charm and personality. Each guest room in this converted Victorian home has been decorated with the romantic in mind. Room 217 has a brass bed and a lacy coverlet; Room 218 has two double brass beds; and all have private baths that are attractively furnished, air conditioning and a quaint café table with two chairs. Breakfast in bed, Continental style, is de rigueur.

Ed is a former electrical engineer, and he and his wife Jane have lived all over the country. About four years ago, during a visit to friends in New Market, they decided that the town needed a good hotel and they were the ones to try it. They started small, as Ed says, figuring that they would learn.

The Rossigs have not regretted their decision. Ed is active on town planning committees and takes a great interest in his new town. Jane, meanwhile, radiates at the thought of meeting and getting to know her many inn guests. As she puts it, "The inn isn't work at all. It's like having friends around all the time."

Room 27, one of three romantic guest rooms at the only inn in town.

The living room at the inn. Antiques abound in this charming 200-year-old town. OVERLEAF: one of western Maryland's finest: Main Street of New Market. Inn is at center, to right of green-roofed building.

THE STRAWBERRY INN, 17 Main St., New Market, Md. 21774; (301) 865-3318; Ed and Jane Rossig, Innkeepers. An 1865 home converted into a 3-guest room inn. Private baths. Open all year. Rates $20 single; $25 double, including Continental breakfast. Children welcome; no pets. No credit cards accepted. Tennis courts nearby.

DIRECTIONS: From Frederick, Md., take I-70 East about 7 miles to Exit 60. Follow signs to New Market. Inn is on Main St.

A 250-year-old inn where no one's in a hurry

In a small town of 750 people, interesting stories have a way of getting around. Often it is difficult to separate fact from fantasy—like the legends about The Washington Hotel, a 250-year-old inn in the center of Princess Anne, Maryland.

Although local legend has it that George Washington slept at The Washington Hotel, many townspeople deny he ever did. But then again, no one is actually certain. And then there's the tale about the dining room ceiling. Designed in Japanese style for the wife of a former innkeeper, the ceiling is a memento to her whimsical ways. It is said that she enticed her spouse to open a Japanese restaurant and then ran off with the Japanese cook.

The double staircase at the rear of the vestibule is another curiosity. The explanation is that one side was for the ladies, whose wide hoop skirts had a way of unexpectedly flying up; and the other half, shielded by a wall, was for gentlemen, who were expected to be above such curiosities as the sight of a woman's ankles.

Antiques are very much a part of this inn, and it is fun to invent stories about how they got there: a Civil War musket, an early electric fan, a large spinning wheel, a seventeenth-century pine sideboard and an early charcoal iron, among others.

The older guest rooms are likely to have some interesting furniture—an antique hat rack or two, an antique desk or chest, a bentwood chair. However, the lights are so dim that the desk is not suitable for serious reading or studying. Room H, a favorite among honeymooners, has a bed with a four-foot, intricately carved headboard that towers over the bed and seems to bless the room. Guest rooms in the new part of the inn have private baths and more modern furniture.

Food centers on such local dishes as hard- and softshell crabs and oysters. Service tends to be slow, but perhaps that is because no one at the inn, especially the guests, are supposed to be in a hurry.

Princess Anne attracts urbanites from Washington, Baltimore and Philadelphia who are escaping from the hectic city pace. Visitors cannot get enough of that small-town atmosphere, and their favorite pastime is to wander around and talk to townspeople and enjoy the old homes and churches. And for the more ambitious, there's Deal Island nearby, headquarters for a sailmaking company as well as a favorite spot for viewing the setting sun.

Left: the infamous Japanese ceiling in the main dining room of the inn is a memento to a former owner who ran off with the Japanese cook. *Right:* honeymoon room at the inn.

Lobby of the hotel. Politicians may come and go, but The Washington Hotel hardly ever changes.

THE WASHINGTON HOTEL, Somerset Ave., Princess Anne, Md. 21853; (301) 651-2525; Robert and Mary Murphey, Innkeepers. In continuous operation since 1744, this 15-room inn is located in a residential town of great historic interest on Maryland's Eastern Shore. Private and shared baths. Open all year. Rates $14 single; $16 to $20 double. Children welcome; no pets. Visa and Master Charge credit cards accepted. The restaurant serves three meals daily. Swimming pool nearby; bicycling is a popular pastime. Historic sites within easy driving distance.

DIRECTIONS: From Salisbury, Md., take Route 13 South to turnoff for Princess Anne. Inn is on main street.

The *grande dame* of Cape May

Located at the southern tip of New Jersey, Cape May is probably the oldest seaside resort in America. Hundreds of years before the Pilgrims landed at Plymouth Rock, the Absecon Indians regularly left their winter hunting grounds to take their ease on the cape's hospitable shores. As early as the 1760s, Philadelphia newspaper ads exhorted their readers to "resort to Cape May," and gambling and horse racing proliferated in the mid-nineteenth century.

Cape May has one of the finest concentrations of Victorian architecture, with all of its variations, to be found in the United States. A showpiece Victorian inn, The Chalfonte is a grand dame who gathers her faithful flock summer after summer after summer. The Chalfonte has style, class and a devoted following who seem to care little that grandmama occasionally needs a new coat of paint or has a dripping faucet. Many of the clientele have been visiting since childhood and now bring children of their own.

The Chalfonte is something like a summer camp, with its offbeat activities ranging from a Christmas in July celebration to a mock celebrity costume party.

But the inn is much more. Because of its striking white gingerbread façade, the inn is a favorite among students of architecture, who volunteer their time every year to help in the repainting—a massive project which is supported by a federal grant.

On the beach, Cape May style.

Showpiece Victorian inn in a landmark Victorian town. **OVERLEAF.** *Top:* from land or air, the red roofs of Chalfonte, at the corner of Howard and Sewell streets, are a distinctive trademark of the inn. *Bottom:* the front porch, a favorite place for congregating. *Right:* a cocktail party in the hotel's garden.

Hotel lobby.

The Chalfonte also appeals to food lovers. The cuisine is Southern cooking at its best, with three generations of Dickerson family working in the kitchen to prepare a different meal every day: Southern fried chicken, country ham and turkey, deviled crab, spoon bread, homemade biscuits and kidney stew are just a few of the best-liked foods.

The inn has been in the hands of one family—the Satterfields—since 1910. The day-to-day management is handled by Judy Bartella and Ann LeDuc, both teachers. Ann, a former U.S. field hockey team member, says that her background has been very helpful in running the 103-guest-room inn. On a good day, Ann quips, she puts in about five miles.

Guest rooms at The Chalfonte are clean and comfortable, but they may be a bit spartan for some tastes. There are few double beds or private baths. Air conditioning is of the old-fashioned variety that is more than sufficient about 98 percent of the time: a cross-breeze from louvered doors to bedroom windows.

During the day, guests love to wander around the wide porches and find a place to sun themselves or get together with new and old friends. The Chalfonte is the kind of place where no one thinks of locking his room—it is just that friendly.

THE CHALFONTE, 301 Howard St., Cape May, N.J. 08204; (609) 884-8934; Judy Bartella and Ann LeDuc, Innkeepers. A Victorian architectural gem with 103 guest rooms. Private and shared baths. Open June 15 to Sept. 10. Rates, single $23 to $31, daily; $127 to $171, weekly. Double $36 to $64, daily; $198 to $352, weekly. 25% discount in June and from Sept. 3–10. Children's rates according to age. Rates include breakfast and dinner in the popular restaurant. No pets. Visa credit card accepted. Ocean beach, bicycling, fishing, sailing, water skiing, tennis and golf nearby.
DIRECTIONS: Take Garden State Pkwy. to end. Continue on Lafayette, turn left onto Madison, right on Columbia, then left on Howard to hotel.

A perfect Victorian country inn by the sea

Tom and Sue Carroll fell in love with Cape May when Tom was stationed at the nearby U.S. Coast Guard station, and they had another inn before taking over the Mainstay, then a museum. By working eighteen hours a day and doing much research into the proper appointments for a Victorian mansion, the Carrolls have turned it into a perfect country inn by the sea. Lace curtains in the high-ceilinged rooms, wrought-iron and brass chandeliers and sconces, Victorian antiques and heavy-framed gilt and mahogany mirrors would indicate the Mainstay still is a museum. The Carrolls say that their guests are so impressed that they take even better care of their rooms than they would at home. The nine guest rooms are large, and each is supplied with a legend about the man for whom it is named: Henry Clay, for instance, was an early champion of Cape May.

The real story of the house is fascinating, too. It was built in 1872 by some Mississippi planters who used it as their own gambling casino. The sweet, gray-haired old lady who always rocked on the spacious, pillared porch was actually a lookout for the police, and when she gave the signal, the gamblers would strike the gaming tables, hide the money in a compartmentalized desk, still in the living room, and be innocently listening to a musicale when the law arrived.

The inn is open only during the summer; Tom and Sue devote the winter months to the endless repair jobs and improvements constantly needed in an old house. In the summer sweet, gray-haired old ladies still rock on the porch from time to time, but they are now guests at one of the showplaces of Cape May.

THE MAINSTAY, 635 Columbia Avenue, Cape May, New Jersey 08204; (609) 884-8690, Tom and Sue Carroll, Innkeepers. A 9-room inn located 2½ blocks from the ocean. Closed from December through February. Double occupancy rates range from $26 to $35, including breakfast and afternoon tea. Private and shared baths. No credit cards accepted.

DIRECTIONS: The inn is located in the center of town, just 2 blocks from Convention Hall.

Left: a twelve-foot mirror in the front hall—Victorian living on a grand scale. *Right:* another grand mirror in the gaming room. OVERLEAF. *Top:* exterior of the inn. *Bottom and right:* recent views of America's oldest seaside resort.

An old barn that looks more like a country club

Camouflaged site: the inn was once a barn which stored grain to feed Washington's troops.

From the outside The Old Mill Inn, with its green-and-white-striped awnings, well-manicured lawn and newly macadamized parking lot, looks like an exclusive country club.

Inside, however, the inn's beginning as an eighteenth-century barn becomes a bit more evident. Beams and cross-beams are everywhere, as well as numerous farm implements and antiques: hayforks, foot warmers, toolboxes, lanterns, wagon wheels, harnesses, and much more. Overlooking the whole ménage is a huge moose head that children have taken to calling Bullwinkle.

Built in 1768, the barn formerly stood across the street by the town mill, which ground grist to feed Washington's army during the winter of 1779. When the barn was moved, not a beam was touched. The main dining room was originally the wagon and machinery room; the bar was the stable; the dining room was used for storing grain; and the seven upstairs guest rooms were the haylofts.

Today, the countryside around the inn has become mostly suburban, with a few neighboring horse farms and several large company offices. People in the area know The Old Mill Inn primarily as a restaurant with a daily luncheon buffet, a varied dinner menu and an international buffet every Wednesday evening. Each week the inn spotlights food from a different area of the world: Africa, New Orleans, the Caribbean, Pennsylvania Dutch country and Central America.

Besides a full complement of American dishes, the inn serves steamship round of beef, as well as such condiments as water chestnuts, hearts of palm, bamboo shoots, papaya, red caviar, loquats and stuffed Greek olives. On the daily menu, the favorites include bouillabaisse à la reine served with linguine and tomato sauce, Russian strawberry soup and the Old Mill grill—baby filet mignon and roast Long Island duckling served with Bing cherry sauce.

Many people who have been dining at The Old Mill Inn for years are surprised to find out about the guest rooms upstairs. The rooms are somewhat small and dark, albeit cozy. Executives who have been transferred to the area often bring their families and stay for weeks on end while they find a new home.

A cozy corner in one of the inn's five dining rooms.

The inn's gardens are the setting for many weddings and special gatherings.

THE OLD MILL INN, Bernardsville, N.J. 07924; (201) 221-1150; Gary Dochtermann, Innkeeper. A 7-room inn in a historic pre-Revolutionary barn, plus adjacent motel with 104 guest rooms. All rooms in both inn and motel have private baths and air conditioning. Open all year. Rates in inn $24 single; $28 double. In motel $34 single; $38 double. Children under 16 in any room, $5 additional. No pets. Visa, Master Charge and American Express credit cards accepted. Lunch and dinner, featuring Continental cuisine, are served in 5 dining rooms in the inn. Swimming pool. Conference center and banquet facilities available.

DIRECTIONS: From New York City, take Holland Tunnel to Route 22 West, then Route 287 North. Exit North Maple Ave. West (2nd Bernardsville exit). Make right-hand turn to inn on corner.

Le Bastard guest room.

Antiques, river views and royal memorabilia

The Black Bass Hotel has been one of the favorite stopovers along the Delaware River and Canal for almost 240 years. It was built sometime in the 1740s to provide Colonial travelers with a safe haven from Indians for the night; and in the nineteenth century, horse-drawn barges plied the canal carrying passengers and cargo. Amenities on board were rudimentary, and travelers were delighted when one of the stops was the Black Bass Hotel, where good food and a hot bath awaited.

Since 1949, the Black Bass Hotel has been the property and passion of Herb Ward, who has taken great care to preserve the feeling of an earlier era. A thoroughgoing Anglophile, Herb has amassed a huge collection of memorabilia about the British royal family through many reigns, and it is well displayed throughout the hotel. The little sitting room off the front hall is a good place to read the paper or, in cold weather, to have a cocktail in front of the fire. The dining room has sweeping views of the Delaware River and an open but roofed gallery with wrought-iron railings for dining out-of-doors. The splendid pewter-topped bar was once at Maxim's in Paris. The kitchen's specialties include a thick and zesty cucumber soup; Meeting Street

crab, made with cream sauce and grated Swiss cheese; roast duck and several interesting desserts. Dining prices tend to be on the high side.

Most of the guest rooms lead out to a balcony with a cast-iron balustrade that runs the length of the upper floor. There guests can enjoy their Continental breakfasts in full view of the surging waters. A two-bedroom suite, with a private bath and its own living room, is the most elaborate accommodation; the other rooms share two baths. Herb has been dabbling in antiques for years, and some of the beds and other furniture he has acquired are prizes. Each guest room is charmingly distinctive; a graceful four-poster with a hand-crocheted bedspread occupies a room with a handsome marble-topped bureau; another room features an ornately carved Victorian bedstead with a colorful patchwork quilt.

George Washington crossed the Delaware just a few miles downstream from the Black Bass Hotel, and much of the history of the American Revolution was made in this area. Herb is fond of pointing out, however, that no George Washington Slept Here sign would ever be found at the Black Bass, since the hotel and its clientele were unwaveringly loyal to the British crown. The father of our country would never have got in the door, much less spent the night.

OVERLEAF: exterior at night, with the River Road in foreground.

BLACK BASS HOTEL, Route 32, Lumberville, Pennsylvania 18933; (215) 297-5770, Herb Ward, Innkeeper. A 6-room inn on the Delaware River. Open all year. Double occupancy rate is $35; $75 for the 2-bedroom and living room suite, including Continental breakfast. Private and shared baths. Restaurant serves lunch, dinner and Sunday brunch. American Express, Visa, Master Charge and Diners Club credit cards accepted.

DIRECTIONS: Located 8 miles north of New Hope on River Road (Pa. 32).

Built in 1794, a center of history and antiques

At The Century Inn, it is not too unusual to find a nineteenth-century spinning wheel in your guest room or a hundred-year-old quilt on your bed. The inn is very much an Early American place, and most of the rooms resemble the best pages of a quality antiques magazine.

Built in 1794, The Century Inn is the oldest continuously operating inn on the National Pike, which is America's first cross-country highway. The inn sits on the crest of a rise, appropriately named Scenery Hill, and on a clear day you can see about thirty miles.

Scenery Hill was founded by the Hill family, who also built the inn. Before the white man came to the area, Scenery Hill had been occupied by the Nemacolin Indians. During the French and Indian War, George Washington and his men frequently traveled along the Nemacolin Indian Trail, which later became the National Pike. As president, Washington again returned to the area, this time to help quash the Whiskey Rebellion, a revolt against whiskey taxes by a rough-and-ready landowners' group at Parkinson's Ferry. One of the front rooms of the inn has a rare Whiskey Rebellion flag.

Other items to see: milk bowls from Albert Gallatin, Jefferson's secretary of the treasury; a 1750 cherry highboy belonging to the Parkinson family that was involved in the Whiskey Rebellion; and the stone ledge by the fireplace in the "common" room, used by the Indians for collecting running water from a nearby

spring. When Nancy Scheirer and her husband, Bob, wanted to repaint the fireplace, they discovered it had had more than fifty coats of paint.

The inn has five dining rooms and serves a traditional but limited menu, including roast turkey, golden fried chicken, stuffed pork chops, filet mignon, and breaded shrimp. The inn's twelve local cooks have introduced many family recipes, including a Ukranian soup of creamed potatoes and asparagus that is very popular.

CENTURY INN, Scenery Hill, Pa. 15360; (412) 945-6600 or 5180; Robert and Nancy Scheirer, Innkeepers. An antiques-filled 6-room Early American inn, formerly a stagecoach stop. Private baths. Open from late March to late Dec. Rates $20 to $24 double; $15 to $17 single. Breakfast served to guests only, but all may dine on fine American fare at lunch and dinner. The inn is located in a resort area with recreational facilities, and there are many historic sites within driving distance. Children welcome; no pets. No credit cards accepted.

DIRECTIONS: From the east, leave Pa. Turnpike at New Stanton and take I-70 West to Route 917 South (Bentleyville exit), to Route 40 East and go 1 mile to inn. From the west, take I-70 East to I-79 South, to Route 40 East, 9 miles to inn.

Fifty-seven coats of paint were removed from the hearth.

The inn is one of the oldest continuously operating hotels on the National Pike.

Golf is the game, Buchanan is the name

The Buchanans have been in Milford, in the foothills of the Pocono Mountains, ever since patriarch George Buchanan first settled here in 1880. He became one of the first judges of the Pike County Court, and some of its early sessions were held in the basement of the Vandermark Hotel, which he also owned and operated. He became a shrewd land speculator, as well, often receiving acreage in lieu of room rent.

Once a capacious 1820 farmhouse, The Cliff Park Inn was refurbished in the early 1900s to accommodate guests, and a nine-hole golf course was opened in 1913 on adjoining land unsuitable for farming. Golf was then a new and little-played sport in America, but 1913 also happened to be the year when an American 20-year-old, Francis Ouimet, won the U.S. Open, beating the two British immortals Harry Vardon and Ted Ratz. Golf became, and still is, the major sporting activity at the inn.

Five generations of Buchanans have lived here, and Harry Buchanan, the present innkeeper, operates the inn in the same friendly, clublike atmosphere of fifty years ago, when guests came by invitation only. It is very much a family-run operation, and each summer the entire clan reopens the inn for their longtime friends and guests. There is always something interesting going on, and the golf course is being extended to include an inland version of the famous oceanside eighteenth hole at Pebble Beach, California. Open only from Memorial Day to November, the main house is frame, painted white, with a spacious front veranda perfect for relaxing in wicker rockers while sipping iced tea. Bowls of fresh marigolds appear every day.

Inside, the main living room is large and homey, divided into separate seating areas set off by Victorian chaises, a plump-pillowed sofa covered in chintz and a games table and chairs by one of the windows. An upright piano covered with a fringed red shawl needs

Guests eat together, family style.

only a lady in a bustle at the keyboard to complete the nineteenth-century tableau. Baths are being added so that each of the twelve generous guest rooms in the main house will have its own, and six cottages tucked around an oval of brilliant blooms offer additional privacy. Hand-crocheted spreads, colorful hooked rugs, organdy curtains, pictures in heavy Victorian gilt frames and hand-painted oil lamps adapted to electricity all contribute to the Old World ambience. Guests may eat together, if they prefer, at the main table in the dining room. Lace tablecloths and bright red napkins are often used, and the full-service kitchen is cordon bleu.

CLIFF PARK INN, Milford, Pennsylvania 18337; (717) 296-6491; Harry W. Buchanan, Innkeeper. A summer hotel in the foothills of the Pocono Mountains. Open from Memorial Day weekend to end of October. Rates include three meals and a day's greens fees. $50 per person per day to $287 for seven days. Visa, Master Charge and American Express. Golf course.

DIRECTIONS: Located 1½ miles northwest of Milford off Pa. 6. Watch for signs to inn.

The 19th hole, overlooking the other 18. OVERLEAF. *Top:* the sitting room, with portraits of Harry Winters Buchanan and Annie Felt Buchanan, 2nd of five generations to run the inn. *Bottom:* guest room in one of the cottages. *Right:* the sitting room.

A mouth-watering menu and ambience that glows

All that glitters is at The Golden Pheasant, a twinkling night spot on the Delaware Canal. The Golden Pheasant has a mouth-watering menu, ambience that glows and overnight accommodations that are a dream. Couples searching for a romantic atmosphere could not do much better than The Golden Pheasant.

The three dining rooms in this 1857 riverside hostelry have cozy corners with intimate tables for two, love seats and high-backed old chairs, candlelight and soft music. The main dining room is a greenhouse, which at night becomes a free-flow of lush, green hanging plants lit by sparkling lights and people huddled in whispered conversations over mahi mahi (dolphin with lemon butter) or some other exotic dish.

Specialties change frequently, but here is a sampling of some of the more intriguing items: pheasant with green grape sauce, plantation quail with peach brandy sauce, sweetbreads with brown sauce and white port, spareribs teriyaki, sanjuck (marinated filet mignon chunks with peanut and soy sauces) and escargots with walnuts and lemon rind, topped by grated Swiss cheese and served over spinach.

Upstairs, each guest is welcomed by a long-stemmed red rose, a thick, thick carpet and a large antique bed. Down the street is the newest addition to the inn, an 1810 brick home with eight guest rooms. It has always been a much admired building among visitors to this Bucks County town, and owners Reid Perry and Ralph Schneider are rightly ecstatic about having it.

Front porch of the inn.

Reid and Ralph have had interesting careers: Reid was a dancer and owner of the Cape May Playhouse in New Jersey; Ralph was an adman. Their musical tastes are eclectic and very entertaining—everything from opera and classical to jazz and soft rock. The inn's clientele, not surprisingly, is sprinkled with people in show business and the arts.

And for airplane buffs, the nearby Van Sant Airport is home for one of the top collections of classic airplane parts in the country.

Gourmet splendor in Golden Pheasant's solarium.

THE GOLDEN PHEASANT INN, River Rd., Erwinna, Pa. 18920; (215) 294-9595; Reid Perry and Ralph Schneider, Innkeepers. Historic landmark inn and nearby Victorian mansion have 12 guest rooms. Shared baths. Open all year except Mondays in summer; Monday, Tuesday and Wednesday in winter. Rates $40 per night, including complimentary Continental breakfast. Children and pets not permitted. Visa and American Express credit cards accepted. Inn is situated between Delaware River and Canal. Canoeing and riding nearby.

DIRECTIONS: From Philadelphia, take Route 32. Erwinna is 17 miles north of New Hope, Pa. and 8 miles west of Flemington, N.J.

Built in 1722, a friendly, intimate inn

One need not travel far to find something historic around New Hope, a 250-year-old town in the heart of Bucks County, Pennsylvania. There is Washington Crossing State Park, where on Christmas Day of 1776 George Washington stole across the Delaware River and crushed the British at Trenton.

There is the Thompson-Neely House, a 1702 building that was headquarters for Washington and his officers before that momentous Christmas. In New Hope itself, there are 180 buildings that date back more than a century. The oldest is the Ferry Tavern, a 1722 building which is today part of The Logan Inn. Located in the center of town, the Ferry Tavern was founded by New Hope's first citizen, John Wells, who operated a ferry service across the Delaware. In keeping with the historic tradition of his inn, it seems appropriate that Carl Lutz, co-owner of The Logan Inn, is now the mayor of New Hope.

In his free time, Lutz would just as soon read a good cookbook as an exciting novel. And because of his gourmet wanderings, he is constantly trying out his food finds at the inn. One of his latest, which he calls

Dating back to 1722, inn is the oldest building in historic New Hope.

loin of pork Logan, is a delightful dish prepared with prunes, oranges, walnuts and ginger. Several of the perennially favorite items on the menu came from his grandmother's kitchen: sauerbraten and Bavarian cabbage, which is marinated for from five to ten days and cooked with ginger cookies and gravy in an old stone crock. The sweetbreads Virginienne, another popular dish, are served with a sliver of ham and sliced mushrooms.

The public areas of the inn are a study in contrasts. The main dining room is large, bright and open. The adjoining bar is small and dark. In the dining room, a two-story glass-enclosed room, people cluster privately, shielded from other groups by some of the largest asparagus ferns in captivity. But inside at the bar, something magic happens and those same private people suddenly become part of a group, talking and laughing with whoever happens to be in the room. Lutz's only explanation is that the bar is just one of those "friendly rooms."

Upstairs, the guest rooms have all recently been redone by the innkeeper. The room with the French double bed is a favorite among newlyweds.

Innkeeper Carl Lutz is mayor of New Hope.

Lunchtime among the asparagus ferns.

LOGAN INN, 10 W. Ferry St., New Hope, Pa. 18938; (215) 862-5134; Carl Lutz and Arthur Sanders, Innkeepers. An Early American inn, with 10 guest rooms, in a quaint town. Private and shared baths. Open all year except for about 4 weeks from end of Jan. to mid-Feb. Rates $30 to $40 double. The popular restaurant serves lunch and dinner. Children welcome; no pets. Visa and Master Charge credit cards accepted. Swimming and tennis nearby.

DIRECTIONS: From New York City, take N. J. Turnpike. Take Exit 10 to Route 287 to Somerville. Take Route 202 South at the traffic circle into New Hope. Look for memorial cannon at inn corner. From Philadelphia, take Route 95 to Route 32 to New Hope.

Delightfully intimate with outstanding cuisine

The Inn at Phillips Mill appears to be one of the very oldest in the area, but although it was built in 1750, it only became an inn in 1973. The little copper pig on the sign over the front door is a reminder that the building was originally a barn next to the piggery on one of the great pre-Revolutionary estates in Bucks County. It was an artist's studio in the nineteenth century and, later, part of a girls' school. Architect Brooks Kaufman and his wife, Joyce, took over the small house and with taste and imagination re-created a charming and authentic Colonial inn with every possible modern amenity. Brooks handled the structural restoration, and Joyce did the interior decoration. The lounge area has a massive leather sofa in front of a large brick fireplace, and drinks or even dinner can be served here in comparative privacy from the other diners at their candlelit tables. A dining alcove can accommodate one group, and Brooks has enclosed a porch with flooring of made-to-order tiles for additional dining facilities. The restaurant is without doubt one of the finest in the area, with minute attention paid to detail and a Continental menu on a par with the best in New York City. The

The reception desk and dried flowers arranged by local horticulturist.

tournedos Henri IV with artichoke hearts and béarnaise sauce is outstanding, and pecan pie with a top crust of brittle chocolate and a dollop of whipped cream is sublime.

Antiques, displays of copper utensils, fresh flowers and collections of old plates decorate the house. The wainscoting and beamed ceilings are the original dark wood in some rooms and painted in others. One of the guest rooms upstairs is too small for a canopied bed, so Joyce has covered the ceiling with a charming fabric to give a canopied effect. A tiny bath has been brightly painted and then lined with mirrors to make it seem larger. In less skillful hands the inn might have been close quarters, but instead it is delightfully intimate. Overnight guests have their own dining room upstairs, and Continental breakfast is left outside their doors each morning in a basket with red napkins, a coffeepot, stoneware cups and warm rolls and pastries in a blue-and-white cloth.

Over the fireplace downstairs is a quotation from the Roman poet Horace: "Ille terrarum mihi praeter omnes angulus ridet" (This corner of earth smiles for me beyond all others).

On his trips between Venusia and Rome, Horace must have found an inn with an atmosphere very much like that of The Inn at Phillips Mill.

A guest room with the morning breakfast basket.

Copper pig is a reminder that inn was once part of a large farm. OVERLEAF: stairway to four very private guest rooms, and the Delaware River Canal, a short walk from inn.

THE INN AT PHILLIPS MILL, North River Road, New Hope, Pennsylvania 18938; (215) 862-9919, Brooks and Joyce Kaufman, Innkeepers. The 5-room inn is located on the Delaware River. Open all year, but the restaurant closes in January. Double occupancy rates range from $30 to $39. Restaurant serves Continental breakfast ($2) and dinner. No credit cards accepted.

DIRECTIONS: The inn is located 1½ miles north of New Hope on Pa. 32 (North River Road).

The original house.

A small family inn with a truly remarkable kitchen

"Our first idea was to be an inn with a small restaurant attached to it," says innkeeper Todd Drucquer. "But somehow it all got turned around. Our family is originally from France, and good food is important to us. So now we have a first-class restaurant with four guest rooms upstairs."

All the better. The Drucquer family opened the Pump House Inn in 1965. It is a perky little cream-colored shingle house with red shutters, and it is very much family run: Todd and his father, Henri, are on hand to greet the guests on arrival, and Todd's two young sons are likely to be around on weekends. The family's collection of ship models and nautical paintings is in the bar, a cozy room with dark paneling and a large fireplace. Digging a foundation for the new dining room uncovered a thirty-five-ton boulder that could not be budged, so it became the foundation of a rock garden with a waterfall and is now the focal point of the room. The four attractively decorated guest rooms all have their own completely modern baths, and comfortable beds welcome the weary traveler.

The Pump House Inn is famous for its food, and

restaurant critics all over the country rave about it. But the most enthusiastic notices come from the dinner guests themselves, many of whom vacation on the American plan at nearby resorts but prefer to eat here. The chef, Mark Kaplan, operates a truly remarkable kitchen, which serves an extraordinary range of Continental specialties. Three styles of dining are available, depending on the day of the week. Bistro dinners feature the hearty food of provincial France, and the table d'hôte is built around a cassoulet or veal Marengo, served family style. The à la carte dinners are more elegant, and the menu might include a delicate pâté, mushrooms stuffed with lobster and crabmeat, a rack of lamb or poached salmon. On Thursday nights during the winter, chef Kaplan's culinary spectaculars make reservations mandatory (and always advisable, anyway). One such feast started with his own creation of escargots in Pernod butter, en croûte, with both Mornay and Bordelaise sauces. The eight courses that followed were highlighted by a smoked trout mousse; lobster and sole quenelles; roast pheasant with sausage, chestnuts, rice, apples and Calvados; and, finally, praline soufflé.

Here is a fine, small country inn with a chef, according to one critic, who cooks, "as if God were watching."

The Continental breakfast.

The innkeepers are great connoisseurs of French wine, some of which is stored in the dining room. OVERLEAF: present-day exterior of the Pump House; the breakfast room; one of the four guest rooms.

PUMP HOUSE INN, Canadensis, Pennsylvania 18325; (717) 595-7501, H. Todd Drucquer, Innkeeper. An intimate, 4-room inn in the Pocono Mountains. Closed over Christmas from Dec. 10 to 27. Closed Mondays from June 16 to October 16. Closed Mondays and Tuesdays rest of year. Double occupancy rates range from $28 to $36, including Continental breakfast. Restaurant serves lunch and dinner. American Express, Master Charge and Visa credit cards accepted.

DIRECTIONS: Located on Pa. 390, 1½ miles north of Canadensis.

Sitting room at the inn.

"A beautiful charming lovely heavenly delightful spot"

Just up the road is the bustling tourist mecca of New Hope, but here at the 1740 House, all is calm. Sandwiched between the slumbering Delaware Canal on one side and the winding River Road on the other, the 1740 House is a tranquil outpost in the trees.

From River Road, the inn appears to be a sunken collection of modern redwood buildings strung out in a loosely connected line. At night, brightened by twinkling lights, that line is a magic glow that begs you to come closer. On inspection, the inn is an artful blending of the old and new—a 1740 barn surrounded by modern guest rooms that all have air conditioning, private baths and terraces, but no telephones or tele-

Looking out on the terrace and the canal.

Nestled away in the woods near New Hope, with all the modern amenities.

vision sets. In fact, the only sound you are likely to hear is the warbling of birds.

The converted barn, which serves as the main building, has two old-fashioned guest rooms and many fine antiques. The building also houses the dining room, where food is first rate—a mixed bag of Continental and American, lovingly prepared and served.

On most evenings, the kitchen serves three entrées, and the avocado soup, rack of lamb, Chateaubriand, spinach quiche and chocolate mousse are particular favorites of guests. The dining room is a small, terraced-in brick porch, and on warm summer nights, you will welcome the breeze from the canal, gently scented by nearby trees.

Canoeing is a favorite daytime diversion among inn guests, who spend lazy afternoons searching for the perfect picnic spot under the trees. And if they don't feel like paddling, they can always enjoy the canal from their private terraces above.

Harry Nessler, the innkeeper, is renowned as a storyteller. A former real estate maven in Manhattan who has traveled all over the world, he never seems to be at a loss for words. When he describes the inn, he likes to call it "a beautiful charming lovely heavenly delightful spot."

Now that may sound like just the kind of thing a real estate man would say, but actually he is not far off the mark.

1740 HOUSE, River Rd., Lumberville, Pa. 18933; (215) 297-5661; Harry Nessler, Innkeeper. A 1740 barn with 24 modern guest rooms. Private baths. Open all year. Rates $41 to $47 with complimentary buffet breakfast. Restaurant serves dinner by reservation. Children and pets permitted at discretion of innkeeper. No credit cards accepted. Swimming pool, rowing and canoeing. (Prices subject to change.)
DIRECTIONS: From New Hope, drive about 6½ miles north on Route 32 (River Rd.).

Youth, talent, ambience and great food

One of the guest rooms.

In the rural heart of eastern Pennsylvania are three young people, busily working to create an inn atmosphere that is absolutely unique. Fred Cresson and Ron Strouse, owners, and Hannah Robinson, a nonfinancial partner, have been at their new venture for a little more than a year, and so far they are succeeding very well.

The cuisine, mostly French and northern Italian, is prepared with the same loving attention to detail that characterizes every part of the inn. The Sign of the Sorrel Horse is becoming a favorite eating place for gourmands from Philadelphia and Allentown, who have been known to drive seventy-five miles round trip just to sample the food.

Among the specialties: salmon Renaissance, with spinach and vegetable sauce, baked in a puff pastry; quail with grapes and cognac; curried chicken with almonds; and oysters Cajun style. The soups are outstanding—consommé with avocado and curried zucchini among them. Chefs Ron and Hannah also make their own ice cream and are trying to perfect a lemon walnut.

Ron encapsulates their philosophy: "We like to challenge our diners to try something different." Meanwhile Fred warns you that the Bloody Mary may be a trifle hot, and he is absolutely right about that.

Hannah and Ron, who both went to the Restaurant School in Philadelphia, prepare the kitchen delights, while Fred makes everything sound so enticing that it's very difficult to choose.

The inn is actually an eighteenth-century tavern that now stands almost in the middle of nowhere. The grounds are a bit bare, but that is 1980's project: a plan for an English garden and a gazebo. Near the inn is the picturesque Nockamixon State Park, with all the usual activities, including sail boating on the lake.

Back at the inn, there is little to do except listen to an occasional car pass by, sip cognac or eat fresh fruit while lounging in a terry bathrobe provided by the management. There are also plants to admire (about six in every room) or antique beds to nap on. The more ambitious can shop the local flea markets or, better still, join in the search for the potter's dump. It seems that the inn's original owner was a potter named Stonback; visiting archaeologists are convinced that somewhere in the area lie the remains of his work.

In a word, the Sign of the Sorrel Horse is a charming, intimate inn that has youth, talent, ambience and great food—a combination that is hard to beat.

Details at the inn are worth noting.

Once a pre-Revolutionary War tavern, the inn serves elegant gourmet dinners.

SIGN OF THE SORREL HORSE, Old Bethlehem Rd., Quakertown, Pa. 18951; (215) 536-4651; Fred Cresson and Ron Strouse, Innkeepers. An eighteenth-century tavern with 6 guest rooms. Private and shared baths. Open all year except Mondays, Christmas and 3 to 4 weeks in February. Rates $26 to $32 double, with Continental breakfast (served in room if desired). Restaurant serves lunch (spring and summer only) and dinner. No children or pets. Visa and Master Charge credit cards accepted. Swimming pool and Victorian garden. Sailing in nearby state park.
DIRECTIONS: From Philadelphia, take Rte. 309 north to Rte. 563 north. Take 563 seven miles to Old Bethlehem Rd. Left on Old Bethlehem Rd. for ¼ mile.

Backwoods country that is beautiful to behold

Starlight, Pennsylvania, is backwoods country that is beautiful to behold. Located 150 miles northwest of New York City and 180 miles from Philadelphia, Starlight is filled with wildlife that wanders freely among the fern banks, moss-covered boulders and farmland meadows. In the evening by Starlight Lake are beavers and wild deer.

Built in 1909 as a summer resort for people from New York and New Jersey, the inn is a rambling green building turned into a restful, year-round retreat. Activities include swimming, sailing, canoeing, fishing, tennis and hiking. Currently, cross-country skiing is the darling of innkeepers Judy and Jack McMahon, who spend their summers marking and grooming the eighteen miles of trails, consulting with cross-country experts, hiking through the woods on neighboring farmers' lands and occasionally having a picnic lunch overlooking Starlight Lake, an effort they are all too happy to chalk off to "research."

The McMahons are refugees from big cities—originally Chicago and later New York. Both had careers in the theater before turning to innkeeping. They describe the inn as "not too fancy, not too rustic, somewhere in between." The McMahons have four children ranging in age from seven to sixteen, and their blond heads can often be seen darting in and out of the homey living room, playing in the game room or sorting through the family's record collection. The McMahon children are friendly and get along well with the other children around the inn.

But no matter what the age of the guest, there is always plenty of entertainment. Judy sits down at the piano or Jack picks up his guitar and everyone chimes in from the cozy fireplace chairs.

The inn's dining room has a simple country look, with plenty of sunlight streaming in through the windows. A German chef originally set up the kitchen, and even though the current chef is from Italy, many German favorites remain, among them Wiener schnitzel and Jäger schnitzel (pork loin, breaded and sautéed with sauce Espagnole, brandy and tomatoes). The inn also serves several chicken dishes, beef and

Site of many evening singalongs.

fish. Breads are all homemade, and coffee is always Colombian and freshly ground. The inn functions on a modified American plan basis.

There are thirty guest rooms in the main house and adjoining cottages. They vary somewhat, but all are basically old-fashioned, with floral wallpaper, chenille bedspreads and organdy curtains. Some of the rooms have been painted imaginatively—in midnight blue, crimson lake or other unexpected hues.

THE INN AT STARLIGHT LAKE, Starlight, Pa. 18461; (717) 798-2519; Judy and Jack McMahon, Innkeepers. A 30-room inn and restaurant on a lake in northeastern Pennsylvania. Private and shared baths. Open all year except from April 1 to Mother's Day. Rates $63 to $69 double; $37 to $46 single, including breakfast and dinner. Special rates for children, ages 7 to 17, ½ rate; under 7 no charge. Pets accepted at innkeepers' discretion. Visa and Master Charge credit cards accepted. Tennis, swimming, boating, bicycling and cross-country skiing.

DIRECTIONS: From points in New York and New Jersey, take Route 17 West to Hancock, N.Y. Take Exit 87 to Route 191, then onto Route 370 to Starlight. Watch for inn signs after leaving Hancock.

Morning greets Starlight Lake—a peaceful spot at any time of day. OVERLEAF: the town of Starlight—49 and still going strong.

*Green Lane,
Pennsylvania*

CANDLEWYCK INN

Rte. 29, Green Lane, Pa. 18054; (215) 679-4171; Max and Elli Gunther, Innkeepers. The oldest portion of this inn dates from 1739, but it is unique for its custom of lighting the windows and interior with hundreds of candles and for the huge flame that burns atop a candlelike silo. Twelve guest rooms with private baths. Open all year except Christmas, New Year's Day, July 4. Single $13; double $15–$18. The Continental-American food served in 4 dining rooms is exceptional, with many unusual entrées, an extensive wine list, and a tempting selection of home-made desserts. Recreational facilities at nearby County Park.

DIRECTIONS: From Pa. Tpke. Ext., Rte. 9, go north to Lansdale exit and turn right after tollgate to Rte. 63. Go north to Rte. 29 and continue to Green Lane. Inn is 1 mile north of town.

*New Hope,
Pennsylvania*

CENTERBRIDGE INN

Box 74, Star Route, New Hope, Pa. 18938; (215) 862-2048; Bob Coburn, Innkeeper. Dating from 1705, this Delaware River inn was once the stopover point on the Old York Rd. between New York and Philadelphia. Nine guest rooms, furnished with an-tiques, with private baths and air conditioning. Open all year. Breakfast served to overnight guests; there's a bar and in good weather dinner is served on a fountain dining terrace overlooking the river; on an enclosed porch when it rains. The large winter dining room has a walk-in fireplace. Children and pets welcome. Visa, Master Charge. Tennis, swimming, rafting, canoeing nearby. Inn is in center of antiquing area, and many points of historical interest are near at hand.

DIRECTIONS: Take N.J. Tpke. South to Exit 10. Take Rte. 287 North, 14 miles to Somerville exit to Rte. 22 West. Go 2½ miles to Rte. 202 South, 25 miles to Delaware River. Cross toll bridge and take Rte. 32 North (River Rd.) 1½ miles to inn.

*East Hampton,
New York*

THE HEDGES

74 James Lane, East Hampton, N.Y. 11937; (516) 324-9807; The Blume Family, Innkeepers. The former Colonial home of the Hedges family, this handsome house dates from before 1770. All the original features have been preserved in remodeling the house into an inn, and the Colonial dining room and furnishings are perfectly in period. The 14 guest rooms have private baths; some have fireplaces. Open May 1 – Nov. 1. Rates $45–$65 per room. Dining room open for breakfast and dinner, with roast Long Island duckling a specialty. The cocktail lounge and dining room are air conditioned, and there is entertainment by members of the Blume family Thursday–Sunday. Children welcome; no pets. No credit cards. Bicycles for use of guests. Main beach 10 minutes walk or by shuttle service.

DIRECTIONS: From New York City, take Rte. 27 to traffic light in East Hampton. Inn straight ahead across from town pond.

MOLLY PITCHER INN

Hwy. 35, Red Bank, N.J. 07701; (201) 747-2500; Michael Kuntz, Innkeeper. One of those hard-to-find and rapidly vanishing small town hotels, the Molly Pitcher is on the banks of the Navasink River Basin. The 110 rooms in the inn and adjoining motel have private baths. Open all year. The superb food, served at breakfast, lunch and dinner, competes with the stunning view from the dining rooms of yachts and sailboats in summer and wind driven ice boats in winter. Rates $27–$34 single; $30–$55 double. Children welcome; no pets. Visa, Master Charge, American Express and Diners Club. The inn has its own dock, and guests who wish to arrive by boat must make advance reservations. Swimming, golf nearby.

DIRECTIONS: From the N.J. Tpke., turn south on Rte. 35 to Red Bank.

OVERLOOK INN

Dutch Hill Rd., Canadensis, Pa. 18325; (717) 595-7519; Bob and Lolly Tupper, Innkeepers. A 19-room inn amid the natural beauties of the Pocono resort country. Private baths. Open all year. Double rate of $72 includes dinner and breakfast. A simple luncheon is served to inn guests only, but dinner, with many unusual specialties and delectable homemade desserts, is popular with area visitors. It is not an ideal resort for children and no pets are accepted. Visa, Master Charge and American Express. Hiking through the beautifully planted grounds is encouraged. Swimming pool, shuffleboard, bocce. Golf, tennis, summer theater, skating and skiing all nearby.

DIRECTIONS: From I-80, go west to Exit 52 and follow Rte. 447 North through Canadensis to first traffic signal. Turn right onto Dutch Hill Rd. ½ mile past the light.

PINE BARN INN

Danville, Pa. 17821; (717) 275-2071; Martin and Barbara Walzer, Innkeepers. A huge 19th century Pennsylvania barn, skillfully restored to retain the original stone walls and heavy beams, is the heart of this hospitable country inn. The 45 motel-style guest rooms with private baths are attractively decorated, and plants and fresh flowers are everywhere. Open all year. Rates $18–$20 single; $20–$26 double. Three lavish meals are served in the 5 dining rooms and a special feature is fresh seafood flown in from Boston twice a week. No charge for children under 18. Pets accepted at innkeepers' discretion. Visa, Master Charge and American Express. The inn is near to three colleges, Susquehanna, Bucknell and Bloomsburg, and advance reservations are essential for college weekends. Golf, tennis, boating and water skiing nearby.

DIRECTIONS: From I-80, take Exit 33 south to Danville. Turn left at first traffic signal and follow signs to Geisinger Medical Center next door to the inn.

REDCOAT'S RETURN

Dale Lane, Elka Park, N.Y. 12427; (518) 589-6379; Tom and Peggy Wright, Innkeepers. A 13-room inn in the scenic Catskills. Shared and private baths. The inn owes its unusual name to owner Tom Wright's sense of humor. A former Britisher, Tom is a trained chef and the menus feature many fine English specialties. Open all year except the first 2 weeks in Nov. and mid-April to mid-May. Rates, $25-$30 single; $36-$40 double, include breakfast. Tom Wright's dinners are justly popular with Catskill vacationers. Children welcome; no pets. Visa, Master Charge and American Express. There's a trout stream on the grounds, and the area abounds in nature walks and hiking trails. Golf, swimming nearby; skiing in winter.

DIRECTIONS: From N.Y. Thruway, Exit 20 North or 21 South. Follow Rte. 23A to Tannersville. Turn left at traffic signal onto Country Rd. 16. Follow signs to Police Center and turn right on Dale Lane.

Hillsdale,
New York

SWISS HUTTE

Hillsdale, N.Y. 12529; (518) 325-3333; Tom and Linda Breen, Innkeepers. This Alpine country inn on the N.Y.-Mass. border overlooks the Catamount ski area. In summer the valley is a riot of flowers, with attractive ponds and a gazebo. The 21 guest rooms have private baths and air conditioning and some have private terraces for enjoying the unparalleled view. Open all year except Nov. Rates, $35-$42 per person, with breakfast and dinner; $28-$48 double, without meals. Three meals daily except May and late Oct. when only dinner and weekend lunches are served. Children and pets welcome. Visa and Master Charge. Swimming in cold brook-fed pond with sandy beach or in warmer swimming pool. Tennis courts, putting green. Skiing adjacent to inn and skating on ponds.

DIRECTIONS: From New York City, take Taconic State Pkwy. to Hillsdale Exit Rte. 23. Inn is 10 miles east.

Easton,
Maryland

TIDEWATER INN

Dover and Harrison Sts., Easton, Md. 21601; (301) 822-1300; Anton Hoevenaars, Innkeeper. After the original inn, long a landmark in this historic area, burned, the present inn was built in Colonial style in 1949. Open all year; rates for the 119 rooms, each with private bath and TV, range from $22-$26, single; $30-$38 double. Suites $38. Three meals served daily in 2 dining rooms, with fresh seafood a popular specialty. A semi-formal dinner dance is held Saturday evening at no extra charge above regular menu prices. The inn also has convention facilities. Children and pets welcome. Visa, Master Charge, American Express and Diners Club. Swimming pool. Goose hunting in fall. Fishing, boating, waterskiing on Chesapeake Bay 5 minutes from inn.

DIRECTIONS: From Annapolis, take Rte. 50 across Chesapeake Bay Bridge into Easton.